KU-663-095

GO QUIZ YOURSELF!

DINOSAURS

IZZI HOWELL

WAYLAND
www.waylandbooks.co.uk

First published in Great Britain in 2020 by Wayland

Copyright © Hodder and Stoughton Limited, 2020

Produced for Wayland by
White-Thomson Publishing Ltd
www.wtpub.co.uk

All rights reserved.

Series Editor: Izzi Howell
Series Designer: Rocket Design (East Anglia) Ltd

HB ISBN: 978 1 5263 1280 8
PB ISBN: 978 1 5263 1281 5

Wayland
An imprint of
Hachette Children's Group
Part of Hodder & Stoughton
Carmelite House
50 Victoria Embankment
London EC4Y 0DZ

An Hachette UK Company
www.hachette.co.uk
www.hachettechildrens.co.uk

Printed in China

Picture acknowledgements: Getty: VasjaKoman cover r, title page r, 20c and 22l, Nadzeya_Dzivakova 5t, 6, 20b, 21t, 22r, 23l and 25t, johnnylemonseed 14l, AdrianHillman 26–27b and 28–29, Yevhenii Dorofieiev 32t, vector 32c; NASA/JPL 8b; Shutterstock: dedMazay cover l and title page l, Amanita Silvicora 4, HappyPictures 5c, 6, 10 and 46, T-Kot 5b, Kapustina Alexandra 7, 10 and 46, Elegant Solution 7, 10 and 46, tn-prints 7, 10 and 46, ideyweb 7, 11 and 47, Zakharchenko Anna 7, 11 and 47, NotionPic 7, 11 and 47, bonezboyz 6, 11 and 47, LuckyStep 6, Iconic Bestiary 7, Chalintra.B 7, Sudowoodo 8t, TrishaMcmillan, Nadezhda Shpiiakina and Egret77 9b, Macrovector 12–13, 16–17 and 27t, ideyweb 12b and 17t, Gluiki 14–15c, Nadzin 14br, Rvector 15tl, Hennadii H 15tr, Pretty Vectors 15b, Teguh Mujiono 18t and 42, Arkela 18b, maxicam 19tl, Taras Dubov 19tr, asantosg 19c, Alfmaler 19b and 23r, Gaynore 20t and 22c, Nadezhda Shpiiakina 21c and 23c, udaix 21b and 43c, Eduard Radu 24t, Jaroslav Moravcik 24b, Tatyana Dunaeva 25t, KatePilko 25b and 48, Ton Bangkeaw 26t, Alyoha 27c, Olga_Belova 30, Maquiladora, AnnstasAg and Nadzin 31t and 34–35, AKKHARAT JARUSILAWONG 31b, Nadya_Art 32b, N.MacTavish 33l, SLKi, Azimuth_A and StockVector 33, NoPainNoGain 36–37c, GraphicsRF 36b and 41t, graphic-line 37t, Best Vector Elements 38b, rvika 39t, VectorPot 39c and 40b, Yauhen Paleski 39b and 42br, nikiteev_konstantin 43t, Blan-k 43b; Techtype 14bl, 37b, 38t, 40t, 41bl.

All design elements from Shutterstock.

Every effort has been made to clear copyright. Should there be any inadvertent omission, please apply to the publisher for rectification.

The website addresses (URLs) included in this book were valid at the time of going to press. However, it is possible that contents or addresses may have changed since the publication of this book. No responsibility for any such changes can be accepted by either the author or the publisher.

All dates in this title are approximate.

All facts and statistics were correct at the time of press.

CONTENTS

HOW TO USE THIS BOOK

This book is packed full of amazing facts and statistics. After you've finished reading a section, test yourself with questions on the following page. Check your answers on pages 44–45 and see if you're a quizmaster or if you need to quiz it again! When you've finished, test your friends and family to find out who's the ultimate quiz champion!

WHAT IS A DINOSAUR?

Dinosaurs were the main land animals on Earth for millions of years. Although dinosaurs eventually became extinct, we have learned a huge amount about them from the fossils they left behind.

TERRIBLE LIZARDS

The word 'dinosaur' comes from two Greek words – *deinos*, meaning terrible, and *sauros*, meaning reptile or lizard. Dinosaurs were a type of reptile, but they aren't related to modern reptiles. Birds are actually the closest living relative to dinosaurs.

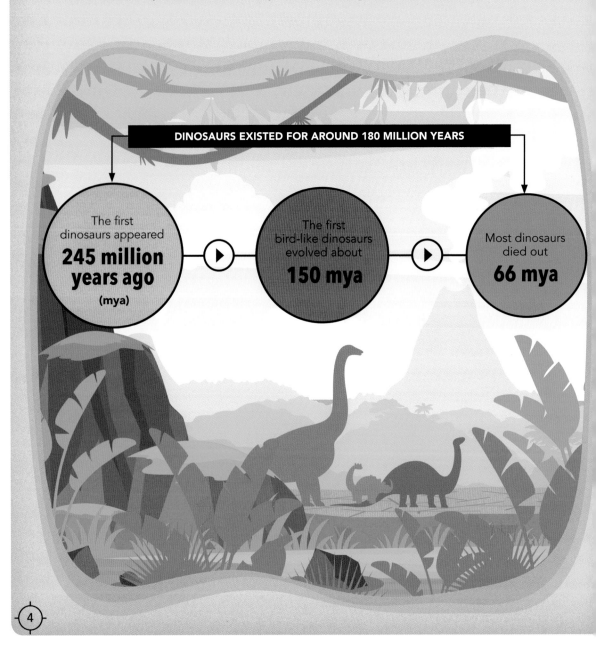

DINOSAURS EXISTED FOR AROUND 180 MILLION YEARS

The first dinosaurs appeared
245 million years ago
(mya)

The first bird-like dinosaurs evolved about
150 mya

Most dinosaurs died out
66 mya

DINOSAUR ANATOMY

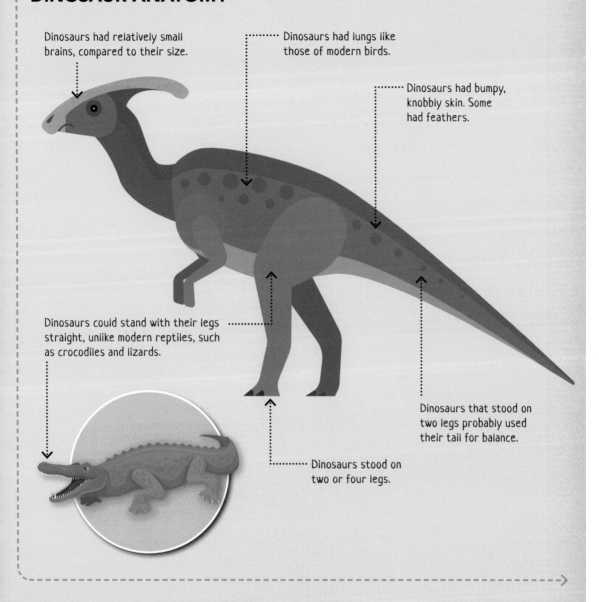

Dinosaurs had relatively small brains, compared to their size.

Dinosaurs had lungs like those of modern birds.

Dinosaurs had bumpy, knobbly skin. Some had feathers.

Dinosaurs could stand with their legs straight, unlike modern reptiles, such as crocodiles and lizards.

Dinosaurs that stood on two legs probably used their tail for balance.

Dinosaurs stood on two or four legs.

OVER TIME

We often think of all dinosaurs living together at the same time. However, that's not accurate. Different species of dinosaurs lived at different times, millions of years apart. Over time, dinosaurs evolved into new dinosaur species and replaced each other.

LIFE THROUGH TIME

Life on Earth started hundreds of millions of years before the dinosaurs. Dinosaurs lived in the Mesozoic Era, but there were many other eras before and after the dinosaurs.

ERAS

An era is a section of Earth's history based on the age of layers of sedimentary rock. Each layer of rock contains fossils of species that lived at that time. Plants and animals were buried by sediment and turned into rock over time (see pages 42–43). Eras are divided into periods.

Although it looks like a plant, this species, *Charnia*, is actually thought to be the first animal.

Precambrian Eon
(4.6 billion years ago to 541 mya)

This period began when Earth started to form.

The first simple-celled organisms appeared 3,600 mya, while the first animals appeared 600 mya in the oceans.

Allosaurus (AL-oh-saw-rus)

Coelophysis (seel-OH-fie-sis) was a late Triassic dinosaur. Dinosaurs from this period were smaller than later dinosaurs.

Mesozoic Era

Triassic Period
(252 to 201 mya)

Most of the land on Earth was one supercontinent called Pangaea, which was surrounded by one ocean.

The first dinosaurs, flying reptiles and marine reptiles appeared, alongside the first very small mammals.

Jurassic Period
(201 to 145 mya)

Pangaea split apart into separate continents.

Large sauropod dinosaurs and carnivorous theropod dinosaurs appeared (see pages 12–13).

The first birds evolved from dinosaurs.

Mesonychid (mess-ON-ee-kid) was a Palaeogene mammal.

Cenozoic Era

Triceratops (tri-SERRA-tops) lived towards the end of the Cretaceous Period.

Cretaceous Period
(145 to 66 mya)

All dinosaurs, apart from bird-like dinosaurs, along with many other prehistoric animals died in a mass extinction at the end of the Cretaceous Period.

Palaeogene Period
(66 mya to 23 mya)

The death of dinosaurs allowed large numbers of different mammal species to develop, including many giant mammals.

Some mammals went into the ocean (whales and dolphins), while others went into the trees (primates).

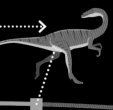

Endoceras

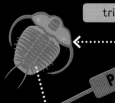

trilobite

coral

Palaeozoic Era

Ordovician Period
(485 to 443 mya)

The climate on Earth warmed and sea levels rose.

The first fish evolved in the ocean and the first simple plants (with no roots, stems or leaves) grew on land.

Silurian Period
(443 to 419 mya)

The first fish with jaws evolved in the ocean.

On land, plants developed veins that carried water around the plant.

Cambrian Period
(541 to 485 mya)

Many animals evolved in the oceans during an event called the Cambrian explosion.

There was no life on land yet.

Devonian Period
(419 to 359 mya)

This period is sometimes called the 'Age of Fishes', as many types of fish evolved.

The first four-legged amphibians evolved from fish and began to adapt to life on land.

Dimetrodon (die-MET-trow-don) is often mistaken for a dinosaur, but it was actually a synapsid.

Dunkleosteus

Carboniferous Period
(359 to 299 mya)

Many species of invertebrate evolved, including dragonflies and grasshoppers.

Amphibians developed further and the first reptiles appeared.

Permian Period
(299 to 252 mya)

Different reptile species evolved and the first synapsids (mammal-like reptiles that eventually became mammals) appeared.

The Permian Period ended with a mass extinction, in which 90 per cent of species were wiped out.

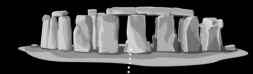

Neogene Period
(23 to 2.6 mya)

The ancestors of humans evolved during this period, at least 4.5 mya.

Most mammals and birds evolved to the forms that we know today.

Quaternary Period
(2.6 mya to present day)

The first humans (*Homo sapiens*) evolved around 300,000 years ago.

Human civilisation began during the Stone Age.

THE END OF THE DINOSAURS

No one knows exactly why most of the dinosaurs became extinct around 66 million years ago. The most widely accepted idea is that a massive asteroid crashed into Earth and disrupted the climate.

THE ASTEROID THEORY

When the asteroid hit Earth, the impact created huge dust clouds that filled the skies. Everything on Earth became darker and colder. Plants died without sunlight, which meant that many herbivores starved. This ended the food supply of their predators, the carnivores.

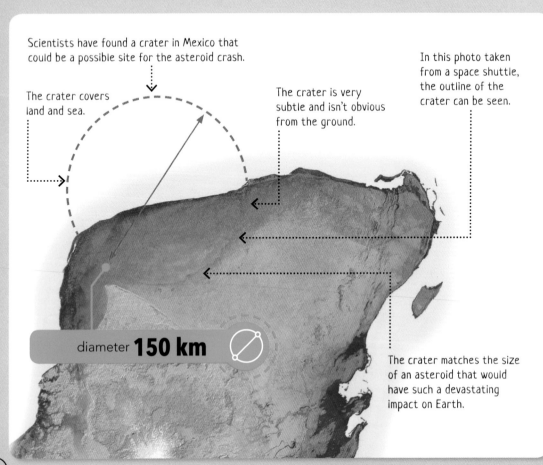

Scientists have found a crater in Mexico that could be a possible site for the asteroid crash.

The crater covers land and sea.

The crater is very subtle and isn't obvious from the ground.

In this photo taken from a space shuttle, the outline of the crater can be seen.

diameter **150 km**

The crater matches the size of an asteroid that would have such a devastating impact on Earth.

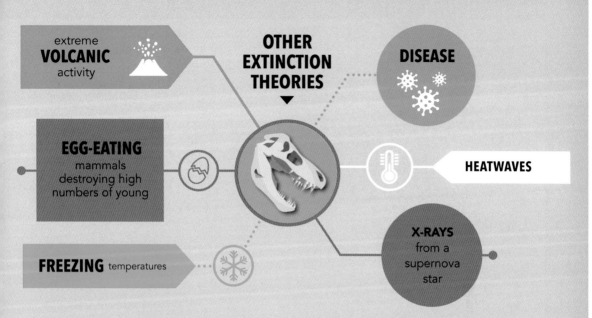

extreme **VOLCANIC** activity

OTHER EXTINCTION THEORIES ▼

DISEASE

EGG-EATING mammals destroying high numbers of young

HEATWAVES

FREEZING temperatures

X-RAYS from a supernova star

GONE FOREVER

Around half the species on Earth were wiped out in the extinction, including most dinosaurs. However, bird-like dinosaurs and the ancestors of most mammals, crocodiles, turtles and frogs survived.

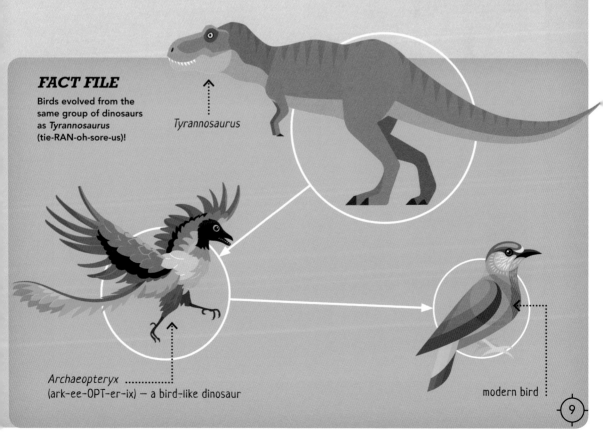

FACT FILE

Birds evolved from the same group of dinosaurs as *Tyrannosaurus* (tie-RAN-oh-sore-us)!

Tyrannosaurus

Archaeopteryx (ark-ee-OPT-er-ix) – a bird-like dinosaur

modern bird

GO QUIZ YOURSELF!

1 Which animals are the closest living relatives to dinosaurs?

2 When did the first dinosaurs appear?

3 When did most dinosaurs become extinct?

4 What kind of skin did dinosaurs have?

5 What is an era?

6 Which species is thought to be the first animal?

7 Name a period that happened before the dinosaurs.

8 Which period is known as the 'Age of Fishes'?

9 What type of animal was a *Dimetrodon*?

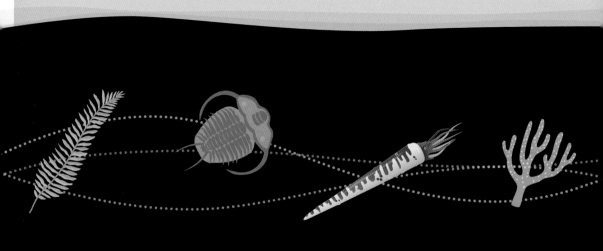

----> **10** What was Pangaea?

11 In which period did the first birds evolve from dinosaurs?

12 When did the Jurassic Period begin and end?

13 In which period did *Triceratops* live?

14 How many years ago did humans *(Homo sapiens)* evolve?

15 In which country have scientists found a possible asteroid crash site?

16 Aside from the asteroid crash, name two other theories about dinosaur extinction.

17 Name an animal that survived the extinction event that killed most dinosaurs.

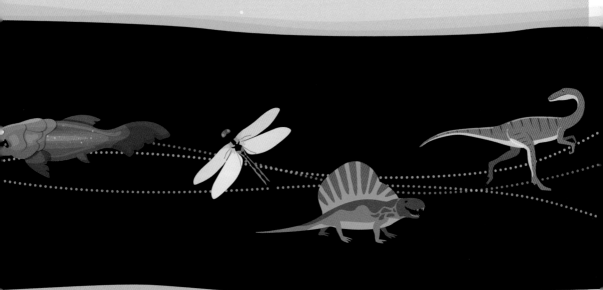

TYPES OF DINOSAUR

Dinosaurs can be divided into two main groups: saurischians and ornithschians. These groups can be split up further into many other types of dinosaur.

Saurischians

★ means 'lizard hipped'

★ includes carnivores and herbivores

Sauropods

★ huge herbivores

★ walked on four legs

★ some of the largest of all of the dinosaurs

★ long necks and tails

Theropods

★ carnivores

★ walked on two legs and had short front limbs

★ three forward-facing toes, like the feet of many modern birds

Tyrannosaurus was a theropod from the Late Cretaceous. Its name means 'tyrant lizard'.

Bird-like dinosaurs

★ evolved from small theropods

★ moved into trees looking for food or protection

★ ancestors of modern birds

Brachiosaurus (BRAK-ee-oh-sore-us) was a Late Jurassic sauropod. It was 30 m long, nearly as long as 2 ten-pin bowling lanes!

Archaeopteryx was a Late Jurassic bird-like dinosaur that was around the size of a magpie.

Dinosaur ancestors

★ lived in the Middle and Late Triassic Periods

★ were small and walked on two legs

Ornithschians

★ means 'bird hipped' (although birds are actually descended from saurischians)

★ all herbivores

★ most had beaks

Ankylosaurs

★ armoured dinosaurs

★ flat bony plates on their back and sides for defence

Ankylosaurus (an–KIE–loh–sore–us) lived in the Late Cretaceous. It had a bony club at the end of its tail.

Ornithopods

★ early, smaller ornithopods walked on two feet

★ as they got larger and heavier, they started to use their front limbs to support their weight as well

Iguanodon (ig–WHA–noh–don) was an ornithopod from the Early Cretaceous. It was one of the first species of dinosaur to be identified.

Ceratopsians

★ horns on the head

★ huge bony frills at the back of the head

Triceratops, from the Late Cretaceous, had a relatively small frill compared to other ceratopsians.

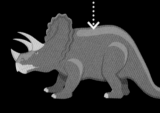

Stegosaurs

★ diamond-shaped bony plates along the back, probably for defence or to attract a mate

★ slow moving as their back legs were much longer than their front legs, so they couldn't run on all fours

Stegosaurus (STEG–oh–SORE–us) lived in the Late Jurassic. It had a spiked tail for defence.

Pachycephalosaurs

★ thick bone at the front of their skulls, which may have allowed them to smash their heads together to fight, just as some rams do today

★ walked on two legs

The skull of the *Pachycephalosaurus* (pack–i–KEF–al–oh–sore–rus), which lived in the Late Cretaceous, was 20 times thicker than normal dinosaur skull bone.

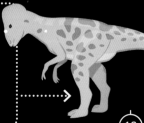

RECORD-BREAKING DINOSAURS

18 m

Dinosaurs were some of the most incredible animals ever to live on Earth. They reached record-breaking sizes and had amazing body parts.

TALLEST DINOSAUR

At 18 m tall, *Sauroposeidon* (sore-oh-poss-I-den) was the tallest dinosaur. It was as tall as 3 giraffes on top of each other. Its huge height was mainly made up of its enormous neck.

LARGEST DINOSAUR

The *Patagotitan* (pat-ag-o-TIGHT-an) weighed over 60 tonnes, which is about the same as 12 African elephants! This makes it the largest dinosaur, as well as the largest recorded land animal. However, palaeontologists have never found a complete *Patagotitan* skeleton, so its size is an estimate based on individual bones. One of its thigh bones measures 2.5 m long!

MOST HORNS

Kosmoceratops (cos-mo-SERRA-tops) had 15 horns and spikes on its head! There were ten on its frill, one above each eye, one on each cheek and one on its nose. Its horns were probably used to attract a mate.

LONGEST CREST

Parasaurolophus (pa-ra-saw-ROL-off-us) had a 1-m-long crest, which measured as long as the skull itself. Tubes inside the crest might have been used as a trumpet to make sounds to communicate.

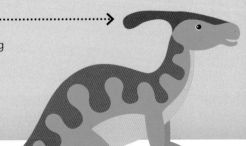

SMALLEST DINOSAUR

Compsognathus (comp-sog-NATH-us) was one of the smallest known dinosaurs, at roughly the size of a chicken! It was also possibly one of the fastest dinosaurs with estimated speeds of over 60 kph.

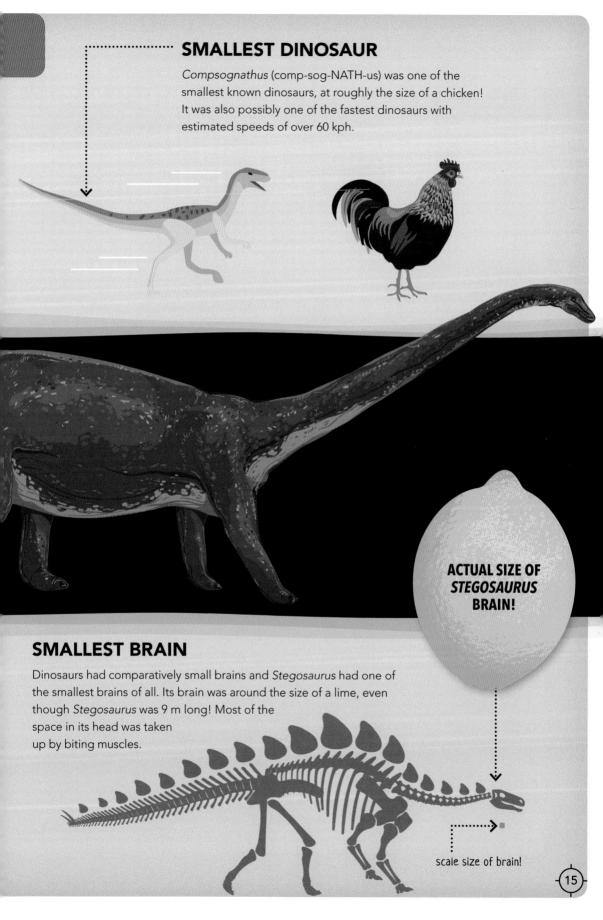

ACTUAL SIZE OF *STEGOSAURUS* BRAIN!

SMALLEST BRAIN

Dinosaurs had comparatively small brains and *Stegosaurus* had one of the smallest brains of all. Its brain was around the size of a lime, even though *Stegosaurus* was 9 m long! Most of the space in its head was taken up by biting muscles.

scale size of brain!

GO QUIZ YOURSELF!

18 What are the two main groups of dinosaur?

19 What diet did theropods have?

20 What does *Tyrannosaurus* mean?

21 Name a bird-like dinosaur.

22 How long in metres was *Brachiosaurus*?

23 What type of dinosaur was *Iguanodon*?

24 Why did ankylosaurs have flat bony plates on their back and sides?

25 Why did *Stegosaurus* move slowly?

26 Which pachycephalosaur bone was particularly thick?

27 Name a feature of the *Ceratopsians*.

28 What was the largest dinosaur?

29 How tall was *Sauroposeidon*, the tallest dinosaur?

30 Which modern bird was *Compsognathus* as big as?

31 How many horns and spikes did *Kosmoceratops* have?

32 Which fruit was *Stegosaurus's* brain the same size as?

33 Which dinosaur had the longest crest?

34 How did *Parasaurolophus* possibly use the tubes inside its crest?

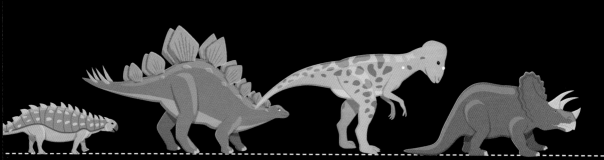

DIET

Different dinosaurs had different diets; some were carnivores, while others were herbivores and omnivores. The easiest way to identify a dinosaur's diet is by looking at its teeth.

huge spiked teeth

strong jaw

CARNIVORE TEETH

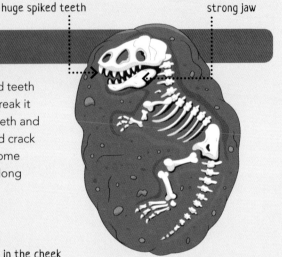

Carnivores had blade-like, serrated teeth that could cut through flesh and break it down into smaller chunks. Their teeth and jaws were strong so that they could crack through the bones of their prey. Some carnivores had pointed teeth and long jaws to snatch fish out of water.

sharp beak

teeth in the cheek for chewing food

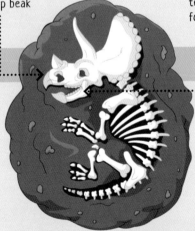

HERBIVORE TEETH

Many herbivores had sharp front teeth or beaks for grabbing leaves. Some had serrated teeth to slice through leaves. Others had peg-like teeth, which acted like a rake, to strip leaves off plants.

TOO MANY TEETH!

The herbivore *Edmontosaurus* (ed-MON-toe-sore-us) had over 1,000 teeth! Its teeth broke down leaves into pulp in its mouth.

SHARP FOREVER

Dinosaurs' teeth constantly fell out and were replaced throughout their life, so they never became blunt.

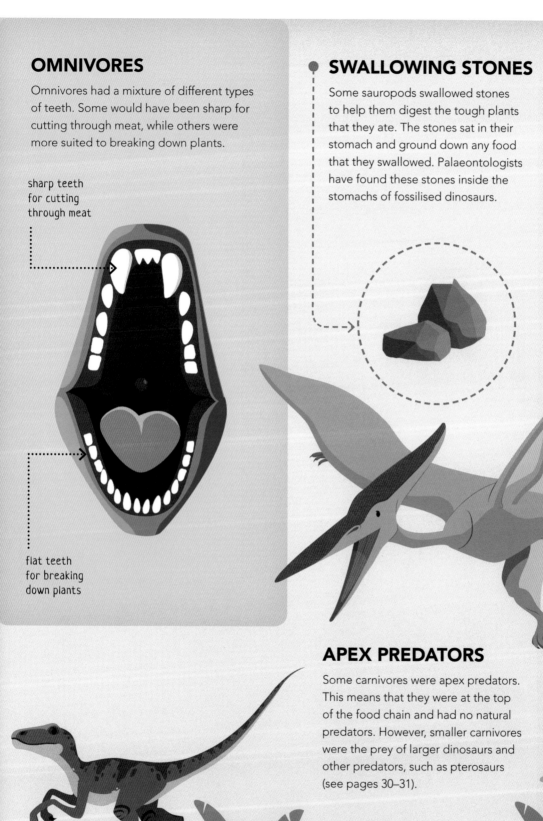

OMNIVORES

Omnivores had a mixture of different types of teeth. Some would have been sharp for cutting through meat, while others were more suited to breaking down plants.

sharp teeth
for cutting
through meat

flat teeth
for breaking
down plants

SWALLOWING STONES

Some sauropods swallowed stones to help them digest the tough plants that they ate. The stones sat in their stomach and ground down any food that they swallowed. Palaeontologists have found these stones inside the stomachs of fossilised dinosaurs.

APEX PREDATORS

Some carnivores were apex predators. This means that they were at the top of the food chain and had no natural predators. However, smaller carnivores were the prey of larger dinosaurs and other predators, such as pterosaurs (see pages 30–31).

ATTACK AND DEFENCE

Fierce carnivorous dinosaurs were skilled predators and were adapted for deadly attack. However, their prey also developed ways to defend themselves and fight back.

DEADLY DINOSAUR ATTACKS

VELOCIRAPTOR (vel-OSS-ee-rap-tor)

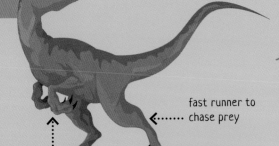

 Time period – Late Cretaceous Period

 Prey – small herbivores

 Length – 1.8 m

giant hooked claw on second finger to grab prey and stop it from escaping ·········

fast runner to ‹······· chase prey

TYRANNOSAURUS

 Time period – Late Cretaceous Period

 Prey – almost anything!

Length – 12 m

a strong sense of smell to find prey

60 teeth (each up to 20 cm long) that could bite through bone; a bite three times more powerful than that of a great white shark

COELOPHYSIS

 Time period – Late Triassic Period

 Prey – insects, small reptiles

 Length – 2 m

hundreds of razor-sharp teeth ···········

fast and agile to help them hunt prey

some evidence that they may have hunted in packs

BRILLIANT DINOSAUR DEFENCE

ANKYLOSAURUS

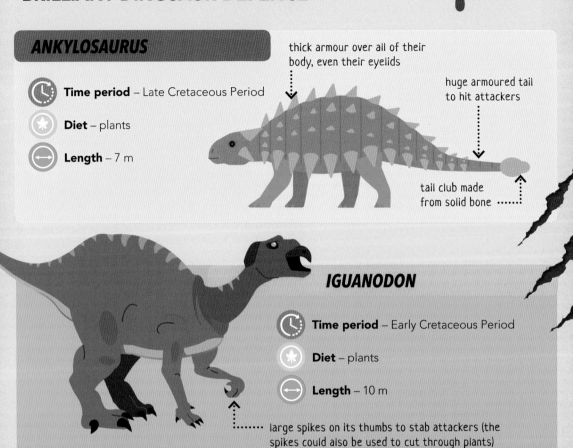

thick armour over all of their body, even their eyelids

🕐 **Time period** – Late Cretaceous Period

⭐ **Diet** – plants

↔ **Length** – 7 m

huge armoured tail to hit attackers

tail club made from solid bone ⋯⋯

IGUANODON

🕐 **Time period** – Early Cretaceous Period

⭐ **Diet** – plants

↔ **Length** – 10 m

⋯⋯ large spikes on its thumbs to stab attackers (the spikes could also be used to cut through plants)

KENTROSAURUS (ken-TROH-sore-us)

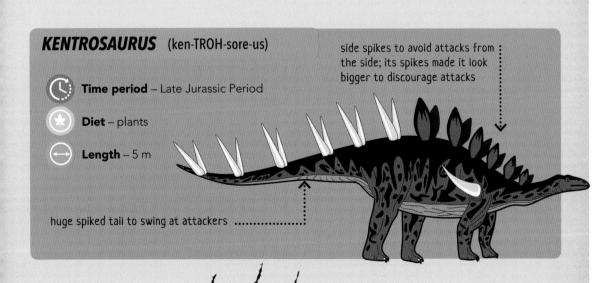

🕐 **Time period** – Late Jurassic Period

⭐ **Diet** – plants

↔ **Length** – 5 m

side spikes to avoid attacks from the side; its spikes made it look bigger to discourage attacks

huge spiked tail to swing at attackers ⋯⋯

GO QUIZ YOURSELF!

35 What is the easiest way to identify a dinosaur's diet?

36 What kind of teeth did carnivorous dinosaurs have?

37 Why did some carnivores have pointed teeth and long jaws?

38 How did peg-like teeth help herbivores to gather leaves?

39 Which dinosaur had over 1,000 teeth?

40 Why did dinosaurs' teeth never become blunt?

41 Why did sauropods swallow stones?

42 What is an apex predator?

43 How did *Velociraptors'* claws help them to hunt?

EGGS AND YOUNG

Palaeontologists believe that newborn dinosaurs hatched from eggs.

DINOSAUR EGG FACTS

Some dinosaur eggs were **COLOURED** and had patterns on them.

The largest dinosaur eggs ever found measure nearly **50 cm** in length!

Dinosaur eggs weren't as super-sized as the dinosaurs. For example, an adult *Ampelosaurus* (am-PEL-oh-sore-us) weighed nearly **7,000 KG,** but its egg only weighed **4 KG!**

Some dinosaurs laid over **20 EGGS** in one nest.

Palaeontologists have found fossilised dinosaur eggs, nests and even embryos.

These eggs came from a *Hadrosaurus* (HAD-row-sore-us)– a duck-billed dinosaur.

They study what's inside the egg by scanning it or by removing the shell with strong acid.

When the first dinosaur eggs were discovered, people thought that they came from giant birds!

NESTS

Different species of dinosaur built different types of nest. Some were open, while others covered their eggs in soil, sand or dead plants. Some species of dinosaur sat on their nests, just like modern birds. Dinosaur nests are often found in raised areas. They may have chosen these places because they were safer. It is possible that they returned to the same place every year to lay their eggs.

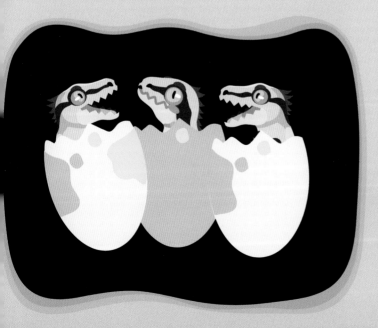

INSIDE THE EGG

Female dinosaurs laid eggs that had been fertilised by a male. One dinosaur embryo developed inside each egg, getting nutrients from the yolk. When the dinosaur young were ready, they broke their way out of the eggs. They were probably able to survive on their own and may not have stayed with their parents for long.

LIVING TOGETHER

Palaeontologists think that some dinosaurs were social animals. They may have lived and hunted together.

FOOTPRINT CLUES

Fossilised dinosaur footprints provide excellent clues to dinosaur behaviour. By tracing the footprints, we can see where they moved and how many dinosaurs travelled together. We can even calculate their speed by measuring the distance between their steps.

ATTACK!

Small carnivores, such as *Coelophysis*, may have also lived in groups and hunted together to bring down larger prey. They probably didn't have any organised tactics – they just all attacked at the same time.

HERBIVORE HERDS

Dinosaur footprints reveal that some sauropods and other herbivores, such as *Diplodocus* (di-PLOD-oh-cus), travelled in large herds. There was safety in numbers, as some could eat while others kept watch for predators. Large groups were less likely to be targeted by carnivores, so the young and injured were protected.

DINOSAUR GRAVEYARD

Around 1,000 *Coelophysis* skeletons have been found in one quarry in New Mexico, USA, which suggests that a very large group lived there together.

GO QUIZ YOURSELF!

52 How were dinosaurs born?

53 What did dinosaur eggs look like?

54 How much did an *Ampelosaurus* egg weigh?

55 How long are the largest dinosaur eggs ever found?

56 How do palaeontologists study what's inside fossilised dinosaur eggs?

57 What did people first think when they found dinosaur eggs?

58 Describe a type of dinosaur nest.

59 Why did dinosaurs often build their nests in raised areas?

------> **60** What role did male dinosaurs play in reproduction?

61 What gave the dinosaur embryo nutrients inside the egg?

62 How long did dinosaur young stay with their parents?

63 What can we learn about dinosaur behaviour from their footprints?

64 How can a dinosaur's speed be calculated from the footprints?

65 Name a herbivore that travelled in herds.

66 Why did sauropods and other herbivores travel in herds?

67 Why did smaller carnivores hunt together in packs?

68 Name a dinosaur that may have hunted in packs.

PTEROSAURS

Pterosaurs (TER-oh-sores) were flying prehistoric reptiles. They weren't actually dinosaurs, but they lived together at the same time.

FIRST FLIERS

Pterosaurs were the first vertebrates to fly and the first animals to evolve flight after insects. Their wings were thin and stretched from their shoulder to their ankle. Pterosaurs may have had fur and feathers. Some were probably warm-blooded (see page 33), unlike modern reptiles.

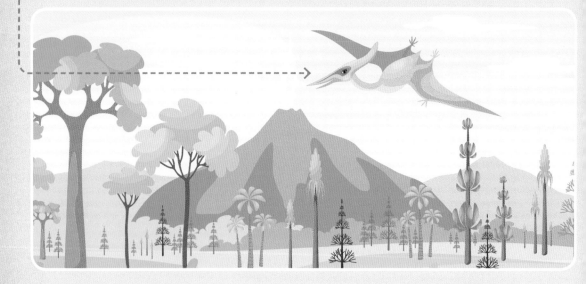

BIG AND SMALL

The first pterosaurs were small – around the size of pigeons. Over millions of years, they evolved to be much larger. Their tails became shorter and their heads and limbs became longer.

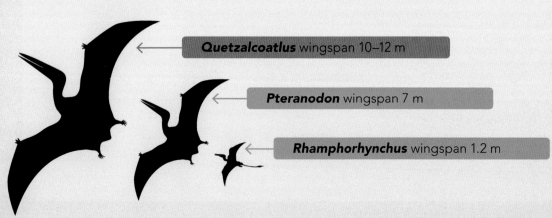

Quetzalcoatlus wingspan 10–12 m

Pteranodon wingspan 7 m

Rhamphorhynchus wingspan 1.2 m

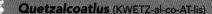

Quetzalcoatlus (KWETZ-al-co-AT-lis)

★ This pterosaur lived in the Cretaceous Period.

★ *Quetzalcoatlus* was one of the largest-known flying animals of all time.

★ At 5 m tall, it was nearly as tall as a giraffe.

★ Its giant jaws measured 2.5 m long.

Pteranodon (ter-AN-a-don)

★ This pterosaur lived in the Cretaceous Period.

★ Its long, pointed crest was probably used to attract a mate.

★ It had a long, toothless jaw.

★ More *Pteranodon* fossils have been found than any other pterosaur.

Rhamphorhynchus (ram-fur-INK-us)

★ This pterosaur lived in the Jurrassic Period.

★ It only measured 50 cm long.

★ *Rhamphorhynchus* had a diamond-shaped rudder at the tip of its tail.

★ Its teeth angled forwards to snatch fish out of the water.

THE END OF THE PTEROSAURS

Pterosaurs died out 66 million years ago, at the same time as the dinosaurs. They have no living descendants.

Palaeontologists have learned a lot about pterosaurs from fossil remains. ·············>

SEA CREATURES

During the Mesozoic Era, many types of aquatic reptiles lived in the ocean. These creatures were related to the dinosaurs, but they weren't dinosaurs.

Ichthyosaurs (IK-thee-oh-sores)
- ★ Ichthyosaurs lived throughout the whole Mesozoic Era.
- ★ They looked like dolphins or porpoises.
- ★ They had very large eyes, which may have meant they had good eyesight to spot predators, such as plesiosaurs.

Mosasaurs (MOZE-ah-sores)
- ★ Mosasaurs lived in the Cretaceous Period.
- ★ They had snake-like bodies, large, strong flippers and long tails.
- ★ Mosasaurs are related to modern monitor lizards.

Monitor lizard

COMPETITION

Different species of ichthyosaur, mosasaur and plesiosaur lived at the same time. They competed with each other for food, such as fish, ammonites and cuttlefish. They also preyed on and ate each other, particularly young or weak animals.

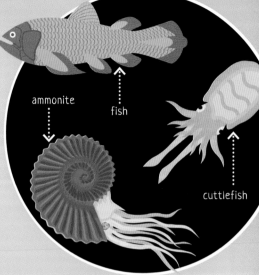

ammonite

fish

cuttlefish

Plesiosaurs (PLEEZ-i-oh-sores)

★ Plesiosaurs lived from the Late Triassic Period to the Late Cretaceous Period.

★ In the Cretaceous Period, plesiosaurs reached huge sizes, measuring 12–15 m, over half of which was their head and neck.

★ One species of plesiosaur is thought to have had the most powerful bite of any animal.

UNUSUAL REPTILES

Unlike modern reptiles, there is evidence that these aquatic reptiles were warm-blooded. They maintained their own body heat, rather than relying on their surroundings to control their temperature. They also gave birth to live young, unlike modern reptiles.

GO QUIZ YOURSELF!

69 Were pterosaurs dinosaurs?

70 Describe the wings of a pterosaur.

71 What size were the first pterosaurs?

72 How large was the wingspan of a *Quetzalcoatlus*?

73 When did *Quetzalcoatlus* live?

74 Why did *Pteranodon* have a crest?

75 How long was *Rhamphorhynchus*?

76 What did *Rhamphorhynchus* have at the end of its tail?

77 When did the pterosaurs die out?

78 Which type of prehistoric sea creature looked like a dolphin?

79 Why did ichthyosaurs have large eyes?

80 When did the first plesiosaurs appear?

81 How long could the biggest plesiosaurs grow?

82 Describe the body of a mosasaur.

83 Which modern animal is related to mosasaurs?

84 What did prehistoric sea reptiles eat?

85 Name one way in which prehistoric sea reptiles were different from modern reptiles.

AMPHIBIANS

Before the dinosaurs, amphibians were one of the first four-limbed animals to walk on land. Their name comes from Greek meaning 'living a double life', as they usually live both in water and on land.

WATER TO LAND

Amphibians evolved from fish in the Devonian Period. Some fish had four strong fins that they used as legs to crawl along the ground. They began to pull themselves on to land. They used primitive lungs to breathe air, rather than using gills like fish.

Tiktaalik (tick-TAH-lik)

★ *Tiktaalik* was a species between fish and amphibians that lived in the Devonian Period.

★ It had gills and lungs.

★ It used its long fins for swimming or to walk on mud.

★ It had a large pelvis that allowed it to walk as well as swim.

WATER AND LAND

Over time, amphibians evolved to be able to spend more time out of the water. However, they still had to return to the water from time to time to keep their skin moist and lay their soft eggs. Eventually, reptiles would evolve to not require either of these things, as they grew scaly, dry skin and laid eggs with hard shells on land.

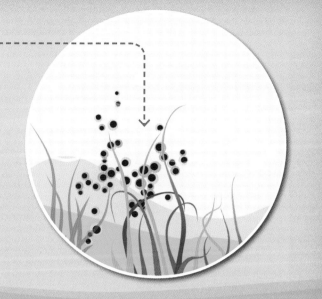

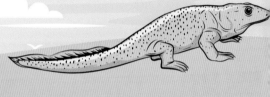

THROUGH TIME

At the time of the first amphibians, there were very few vertebrates on land. Amphibians had plenty of food to eat, including plants and insects, and fish from the water. Later, during the Mesozoic Era, some species became extinct. Other species survived, including the ancestors of modern reptiles, such as frogs and salamanders.

Eryops (EAR-ee-ops)

★ *Eryops* was a large amphibian from the Permian Period.

★ Measuring 2 m long, it was one of the largest land animals at that time.

★ It ate mostly fish and other small animals.

★ Its hip structure from fossils shows that it would have been good at walking on land.

EARLY MAMMALS

The first mammals appeared in the Triassic Period. During the Age of the Dinosaurs, mammals remained small, but afterwards, they grew to huge sizes.

MESOZOIC MAMMALS

Most mammals that lived at the same time as the dinosaurs were the size of small rodents, such as rats. They were herbivores or insectivores (ate only insects). There were a few exceptions, such as *Repenomamus* (rep-en-o-MAH-mus), which was roughly the size of a badger and hunted vertebrates, including baby dinosaurs.

EGGS AND YOUNG

Mammals have always fed their young on milk, but they developed various forms of giving birth over time. The first mammals laid eggs, like the reptiles that they evolved from. Some mammals, such as the platypus and the echidna still lay eggs today. Later, mammals evolved to give birth to very small, live young. They kept them in pouches like kangaroos. After that, mammals began to give birth to more developed young, like most do today.

Megazostrodon
(meg-ah-ZOSS-troh-don)

- ★ *Megazostrodon* lived in the Late Triassic Period.
- ★ It was one of the first mammals.
- ★ It was the size of a shrew, around 10–12 cm long, and had a furry body.
- ★ *Megazostrodon* was nocturnal – probably to avoid reptile predators that were active during the day.

SURVIVAL

Mammals were better equipped to survive the extinction event that we believe to have killed the dinosaurs. They were much smaller, so they didn't need as much food to survive. Their fur coats kept them warm in the cold climate.

GETTING BIGGER

Over time, mammals grew in size and took the place of the dinosaurs as the largest animals on Earth. Huge ancestors of modern animals, such as armadillos, anteaters and sloths evolved. However, many of these large mammals died out in the last Ice Age, around 11,500 years ago.

Megatherium
(meg-ah-THEER-ee-um)

★ *Megatherium* lived during the Quaternary Period, which means that it overlapped with human ancestors.

★ It was related to modern sloths, but was 10 times larger than them.

★ *Megatherium* weighed up to 4 tonnes, which is the same as a male Asian elephant.

★ It measured 3.5 metres tall when standing on its hind legs.

★ It had long arms and large claws to pull branches down to its mouth.

Glyptodon (GLIP-toe-don)

★ *Glyptodon* lived in the Quaternary Period.

★ It was related to modern armadillos, but much larger – around the same size and shape as a Volkswagen Beetle car.

★ *Glyptodon* looked a bit like a turtle, with a huge domed shell made up of bony plates.

★ Its shell measured 1.5 m long, making up around half of its length.

★ It had an armoured tail with bony spikes that was used as a weapon.

GO QUIZ YOURSELF!

86 Why are amphibians said to lead a double life?

87 In which period did amphibians evolve from fish?

88 How did the first amphibians breathe on land?

89 How did *Tiktaalik* move?

90 Why do amphibians need to return to the water?

91 Name one way in which reptiles have evolved to not need water.

92 How long was *Eryops*?

93 What did *Eryops* eat?

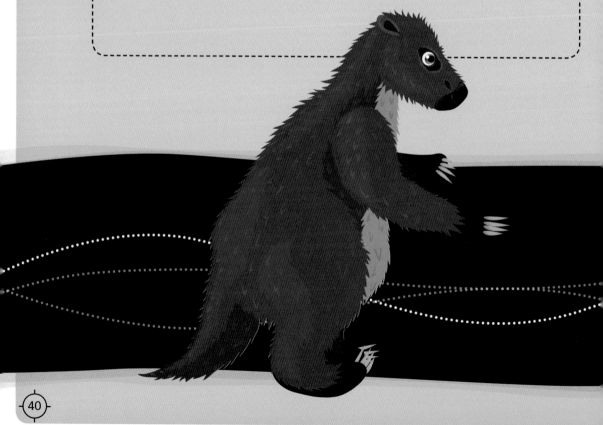

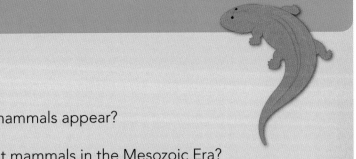

----→ **94** When did the first mammals appear?

95 What size were most mammals in the Mesozoic Era?

96 Why were mammals such as *Megazostrodon* nocturnal?

97 Name two different ways that mammals have given birth.

98 Name one reason why mammals were better equipped to survive the extinction event than dinosaurs.

99 When did many large mammals die out?

100 Which modern animal is *Megatherium* related to?

101 How tall was *Megatherium*?

102 Which body part did *Glyptodon* use to attack predators?

DISCOVERING DINOSAURS

Everything that we know about dinosaurs and prehistoric living things comes from fossils (remains preserved in rock).

HISTORY

Up until the late seventeenth century, no one realised that the animals of today hadn't been around forever, and that different animals – including dinosaurs – even existed. In the eighteenth century, people started to collect and study fossils and identified dinosaur species. This led to a huge explosion in the understanding of prehistoric life.

Palaeontologists use different tools to uncover dinosaur fossils.

They use shovels and picks to break through the top layers of rock.

As they get closer to the bones, they use smaller rock hammers and tiny knives and chisels.

They use paintbrushes to keep the area clean, as it's best not to touch the fossils as oils in the skin can damage the fossils.

Palaeontologists use glue to stabilise the fossils and stick them back together if they crumble.

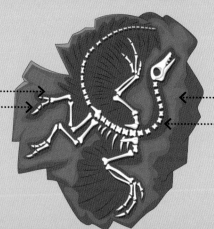

HOW ARE FOSSILS FORMED?

Fossils only form when living things are buried by mud or sediment after they die. For this reason, fossils of land animals are rare.

1 A dinosaur dies in a river and sinks to the bottom.

2 The dinosaur's flesh decomposes and its skeleton is covered with sediment.

3 Water seeps through the sediment. Minerals from the water replace the bones and they harden and turn into a fossilised rock.

4 Layers of sediment build up above the skeleton and turn into rock.

5 The movement of Earth's crust means that the land above the fossil is no longer below water.

6 Rock erodes above the fossil, revealing it to palaeontologists.

TYPES OF FOSSIL

There are many types of fossil.

<····· **Preserved in amber (fossilised tree resin)**

Insects and small animals were sometimes trapped in the resin when it was fresh and sticky. They were preserved inside as the amber hardened.

FOSSIL FAECES

A piece of fossilised dung is called a coprolite. One of the longest coprolites ever found measured over 1 m long!

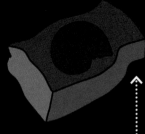

Cast

A cast fossil begins like a mould fossil with an imprint left in soft mud. Then, minerals build up in the space left behind and harden, creating a cast of the original shape.

Mould ·····

An imprint of an animal or plant is left in soft mud, which later hardens into rock. The living thing decomposes but its imprint is left behind.

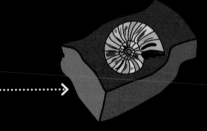

Trace fossil

These are fossils that provide evidence about how prehistoric animals lived, such as their footprints, nests, dung and eggs.

QUIZ TIME!

After you've finished testing yourself, why not use this book to make a quiz to test your friends and family? You could take questions from each section to make different rounds, or mix and match across the book for a general knowledge dinosaur quiz. You can even make up your own quiz questions! Use these dinosaur fossil facts to get you started. For example, **'What is a trace fossil?** or **'Why are fossils of land animals rare?'**

ANSWERS

1 Birds

2 245 million years ago

3 66 million years ago

4 Bumpy, knobbly skin and some had feathers

5 A section of Earth's history based on the age of layers of sedimentary rock

6 *Charnia*

7 The Cambrian, Ordovician, Silurian, Devonian, Carboniferous or the Permian

8 The Devonian Period

9 A synapsid (a mammal-like reptile)

10 A supercontinent of all the land on Earth during the Triassic Period

11 The Jurassic Period

12 201 to 145 million years ago

13 The Cretaceous Period

14 Around 300,000 years ago

15 Mexico

16 Disease, extreme volcanic activity, heatwaves, freezing temperatures, X-rays from a supernova star or egg-eating mammals destroying high numbers of young

17 Bird-like dinosaurs and the ancestors of most mammals, crocodiles, turtles and frogs

18 Saurischians and ornithschians

19 Carnivorous

20 Tyrant lizard

21 *Archaeopteryx*

22 30 m long

23 Ornithopod

24 For defence

25 Their back legs were much longer than their front legs, so they couldn't run on all fours

26 Skull

27 Horns and huge bony frills on the head

28 *Patagotitan*

29 18 m

30 A chicken

31 15 horns and spikes

32 A lime

33 *Parasaurolophus*

34 As a trumpet to make sounds to communicate

35 Look at its teeth

36 Blade-like, serrated teeth

37 To snatch fish out of water

38 They worked like a rake to strip leaves off plants

39 *Edmontosaurus*

40 Because they constantly fell out and were replaced throughout their life

41 To help them digest tough plants

42 A predator at the top of the food chain with no natural predators

43 They had a giant hooked claw on each hand to grab prey and stop it from escaping

44 60 teeth

45 Their sense of smell

46 12 m long

47 Insects and small reptiles

48 Solid bone

49 Stabbing them with its large thumb spikes

50 Herbivorous (plants)

51 With spikes on its sides

52 Newborn dinosaurs hatched from eggs

53 Some were coloured and patterned

54 4 kg

55 50 cm long

56 By scanning them or by removing the shells with strong acid

57 That they came from giant birds

58 Open, or covered with soil, sand or dead leaves

59 They were safer

60 They fertilised the eggs

61 The egg yolk

62 Not for long, they were probably able to survive on their own as soon as they hatched

63 Where they went and how many dinosaurs travelled together

64 By measuring the distance between the steps

65 *Diplodocus*

66 To protect them against predators

67 To bring down larger prey

68 *Coelophysis*

69 No, they were reptiles, but not dinosaurs

70 Thin wings that stretched from the shoulder to the ankle

71 Small – around the size of a pigeon

72 10–12 m

73 The Cretaceous Period

74 Probably to attract a mate

75 50 cm long

76 A diamond-shaped rudder

77 66 million years ago, along with the dinosaurs

78 Ichthyosaurs

79 To spot predators

80 The Late Triassic Period

81 12–15 m long

82 A snake-like body with large, strong flippers and a long tail

83 The monitor lizard

84 Fish, ammonites, cuttlefish and each other

85 They were warm-blooded and gave birth to live young

86 Because they live in water and on land

87 The Devonian Period

88 With primitive lungs

89 It swam and walked on land

90 To keep their skin moist and lay eggs

91 Scaly, dry skin and laying eggs with hard shells

92 2 m long

93 Fish and other small animals

94 The Triassic Period

95 Around the size of small rodents

96 To avoid reptile predators that were active during the day

97 Laying eggs, giving birth to very small young that live in pouches or giving birth to developed young

98 They didn't need as much food and they had fur to keep them warm

99 In the last Ice Age, around 11,500 years ago

100 The sloth

101 3.5 m tall

102 Its armoured tail with bony spikes

HOW WELL DID YOU DO?

100–102 --→ QUIZMASTER

75–99 -----→ QUIZTASTIC

50–74 ------→ QUIZ ON

25–49 -------→ QUIZLING

0–24 --------→ QUIZ IT AGAIN

GLOSSARY

amber – fossilised tree resin

ammonite – a prehistoric sea creature with a flat, spiral shell

asteroid – a large space rock that orbits the Sun

carnivore – an animal that only eats meat

crater – a round hole in the ground, usually caused by space rocks crashing into it

embryo – a developing animal that is not ready to be born

eon – a period of time that is so long that it can't be measured

era – a period of Earth's history based on the age of layers of sedimentary rock

evolve – to change and develop gradually over time

fossil – the shape of something that has been preserved in rock for a very long time

gills – the organ with which fish and some other water animals breathe

herbivore – an animal that only eats plants

herd – a large group of animals that live and feed together

Ice Age – a period of time during which the temperature on Earth drops very low

mass extinction – a period in which many species of living thing die out forever

mate – a reproductive partner

omnivore – an animal that eats meat and plants

palaeontologist – someone who studies dinosaurs and prehistoric life

period – a length of time within an era

sediment – small pieces of sand, mud and stones

sedimentary rock – rock that forms from layers of sediment being pressed together over time

serrated – with a row of sharp points

vertebrate – an animal with a backbone, such as a fish or a mammal

warm-blooded – describes an animal that can control its own body temperature and does not need to change environment to warm up or cool down

wingspan – the distance between the tips of the wings of an animal

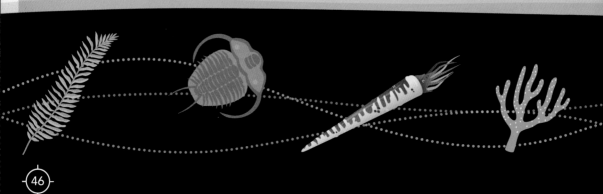

FURTHER INFORMATION

 BOOKS

Birth of the Dinosaurs (Planet Earth)
by Michael Bright (Wayland, 2016)

Dinosaurs (Prehistoric Life)
by Claire Hibbert (Franklin Watts, 2019)

Dinosaur Infosaurus series
by Katie Woolley (Wayland, 2018)

 WEBSITES

www.nhm.ac.uk/discover/dino-directory.html
Find out fun facts about different dinosaurs in the Dino Directory.

www.natgeokids.com/uk/play-and-win/games/dinosaur-memory/
Test your memory with a dinosaur quiz.

www.dkfindout.com/uk/dinosaurs-and-prehistoric-life/
Discover amazing facts and information about dinosaurs and prehistoric life.

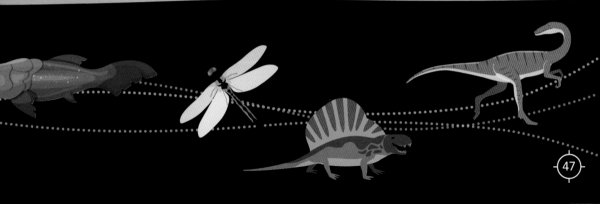

INDEX

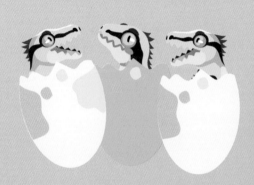

More titles in the the
Go Quiz Yourself! series

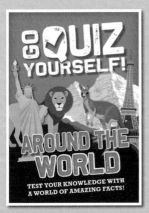

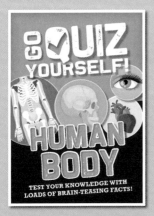

EDGE
BOOKS

MONSTER HANDBOOK

KU-131-883

VAMPIRES

The Truth Behind
HISTORY'S CREEPIEST BLOODSUCKERS

by Alicia Z. Klepeis

raintree
a Capstone company — publishers for children

Raintree is an imprint of Capstone Global Library Limited, a company incorporated in England and Wales having its registered office at 7 Pilgrim Street, London, EC4V 6LB – Registered company number: 6695582

www.raintree.co.uk
myorders@raintree.co.uk

Text © Capstone Global Library Limited 2016
The moral rights of the proprietor have been asserted.

All rights reserved. No part of this publication may be reproduced in any form or by any means (including photocopying or storing it in any medium by electronic means and whether or not transiently or incidentally to some other use of this publication) without the written permission of the copyright owner, except in accordance with the provisions of the Copyright, Designs and Patents Act 1988 or under the terms of a licence issued by the Copyright Licensing Agency, Saffron House, 6–10 Kirby Street, London EC1N 8TS (www.cla.co.uk). Applications for the copyright owner's written permission should be addressed to the publisher.

Edited by Aaron Sautter
Designed by Bobbie Nuytten
Picture research by Gina Kammer
Production by Laura Manthe
Printed in China

ISBN 978 1 4747 0446 5
19 18 17 16 15
10 9 8 7 6 5 4 3 2 1

British Library Cataloguing in Publication Data
A full catalogue record for this book is available from the British Library.

Acknowledgements
Alamy: © Jack Carey, 21; Bridgeman Images: Pictures From History/Philippines: An aswang or vampire-like mythical creature of the Philippines as represented by Juan de Plazcensia in the late 15th century, 8, Private Collection/Dracula Claims Lucy, 2009 (oil on canvas), Barry, Jonathan (Contemporary Artist), 5; Corbis: 10, © Bettmann, 17, 25, © John Springer Collection, 28, © Leemage, 18; Getty Images: Hulton Archive, 23; Granger, NYC: ullstein bild, 15; Newscom: Album/20TH CENTURY FOX TV, 26, KRT/RON COHEN, 29, ZUMA Press/Ropi/Boma, 12; Science Source: 13; Shutterstock: Alexey Painter, cover, Alexey Painter, 4, Fabiana Ponzi, 27, Ginger Ale, (bats) 29, Golubentsev, 7, hagit berkovich, 6, JMicic, (hands) 9, Lasha Kilasonia, (Earth map) 9, MaraZe, 16, Michael Wick, 19, Radek Sturgolewski, 24, Sarun T, 14, Taeya18, 30, Zacarias Pereira da Mata, cover, 1

Design Elements
Shutterstock: blue pencil (calligraphic designs), Ensuper (grunge background), Gordan (grunge frames), Slava Gerj (grunge scratched background)

We would like to thank David Gilmore, Professor of Anthropology at Stony Brook University, New York, for his invaluable help in the preparation of this book.

Every effort has been made to contact copyright holders of material reproduced in this book. Any omissions will be rectified in subsequent printings if notice is given to the publisher.

All the internet addresses (URLs) given in this book were valid at the time of going to press. However, due to the dynamic nature of the internet, some addresses may have changed, or sites may have changed or ceased to exist since publication. While the author and publisher regret any inconvenience this may cause readers, no responsibility for any such changes can be accepted by either the author or the publisher.

Contents

Scary, undead bloodsuckers

Night is approaching. Darkness closes in over a crumbling old castle. Slowly, a coffin opens. A shadowy mist emerges and floats towards an open window. In an instant, the mist transforms into a huge black bat that flies off towards the nearby village. What is this monstrous creature? It's a vampire – and it's looking for a fresh meal of blood!

Vampire legends describe the monsters as terrifying, **undead** creatures of the night. Vampires in today's books and films are often handsome men or beautiful women. But vampire stories through history usually described them as frightening and cunning monsters. They were technically dead, but still prowled around at night hunting for fresh blood. Vampires in several tales even had the power to **hypnotize** their victims, making them easy prey. Take a walk through history and see how stories about these scary monsters have changed over time.

undead no longer alive but still able to move and take action

hypnotize to put a person into a sleep-like state

In many tales, bloodsucking vampires enjoy hypnotizing and feeding on the blood of young women.

CHAPTER 1
Vampires in the ancient world

Bloodsucking vampires have lived in people's imaginations for thousands of years. People in the ancient world often blamed vampires for diseases, unnatural deaths and other events they didn't understand. In ancient stories about vampires, these undead monsters spread fear and chaos wherever they went.

THE FIRST VAMPIRES

Many people believe the first vampire myths began in ancient Babylon. The Babylonians believed in a female demon called *Lilitu*. This creature was said to be the bearer of disease, illness and death. It usually looked like a normal human woman. But it had a nasty habit of feasting on the blood of babies.

FACT: The *otgiruru* from Namibian legends was a vampire-like dog. Sometimes it howled and pretended to be a family pet that was injured. When someone came to its aid, the creature viciously attacked the person.

The ancient Assyrians believed in bloodthirsty monsters called *ekimmu*. These creatures were thought to be the restless spirits of people who died violently or who weren't buried properly. Some *ekimmu* were described as thin, sickly people. But others supposedly appeared as winged demons or simply as rushing wind. *Ekimmu* were thought to drink the blood of people who were near death.

Stories from ancient Greece and Rome featured terrifying monsters called *strix*. Blocking a *strix* from a person's home was said to be impossible. Legends stated that no barriers or locks could keep them out. These terrible creatures usually flew around at night, looking for children to attack.

Strix *were said to be female shape-shifters that could turn into birds of prey such as owls.*

ANCIENT ASIAN VAMPIRES

Ancient Asian **folklore** featured several types of scary bloodsucking monsters. *Aswangs* were shape-shifting vampires from stories told in the Philippines. By day they usually looked like beautiful young women. But at night they often turned into animals such as large birds, bats or dogs. These creatures enjoyed eating the bloody hearts and livers of their victims.

The *churel* from India was a gruesome creature. Its feet were turned backwards, with the toes at the back and the heel at the front. Many stories described a *churel* as a woman who died during childbirth. This creature sometimes appeared as a beautiful woman to trap its victims. Young men were especially powerless against a *churel's* charms.

folklore tales, sayings and customs among a group of people

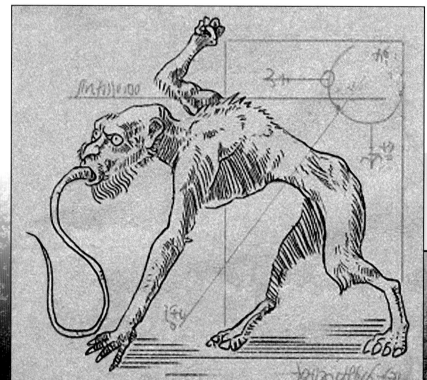

Aswangs *were said to use long, pointed tongues to pierce people's necks and drink their blood.*

ROME
strix
shape-shifter that turned into a bird of prey; supposedly no barriers or locks on doors could keep them out

GREECE/ROME
lamia
half woman and half snake; sucked the blood of men

BABYLON
Lilitu
a demon that appeared as a human woman; drank the blood of babies

ASSYRIA
ekimmu
appeared as sickly people, winged demons or rushing wind; drank the blood of people near death

CHINA
jiang-shi
strong and vicious, had super-long eyebrows used to magically trap victims

PHILIPPINES
aswang
could turn into a bird and hide in trees; long, pointed tongue could prick a victim's neck from a long distance away

GREECE
keres (Ceres)
preyed on sick people; grabbed victims with large claws or talons; were said to escape from jars used to hold the bodies of the dead

INDIA
churel
feet were backwards with heel at the front and toes at the back; their beauty easily attracted male victims

MALAYSIA
langsuir
female vampire that sucked blood through a hole in the back of its neck; preferred to drink babies' blood

AUSTRALIA
yara-ma-yha-who
hid in fig trees to attack people who camped under them

CHAPTER 2

Medieval vampire folklore

In the Middle Ages (c. AD 500 to 1450), most people were uneducated and understood little about death. During this period the **plague** killed millions of people across Europe. With imaginations running wild, people often believed that vampires were responsible for so much death and suffering.

Also known as the Black Death, tens of millions of people across Europe died from the plague in the mid-1300s.

FACT: Sometimes people with a disease called rabies were thought to be vampires. Infected people often had red foam on their lips. Medieval people thought this was because the infected people had just dined on blood. But we now know the red foam came from excess saliva.

MISTAKEN FOR VAMPIRES

A dead body's appearance may have led some **medieval** people to believe in vampires. A dead body can become bloated from a build-up of gases inside it. The gases can also force blood to trickle out of the body's eyes, nose or mouth. It's easy to see how medieval people could make mistakes about such bloody, bloated bodies. They often thought the bodies were vampires who had just fed on living people's blood.

Dead bodies had other signs that led people to mistake them for vampires. When a body **decomposes**, its skin shrinks back as it dries out. This process causes the hair and teeth to appear to grow longer. These "signs of life" helped to convince believers that the bodies were vampires who had cheated death.

plague disease that spreads quickly and kills most people who catch it

medieval having to do with the period of European history between AD 500 and 1450

decompose to rot or decay

BECOMING A VAMPIRE

According to medieval stories, there were many ways people could become vampires. In some places it was thought that people could be born as vampires. In Russia, if a baby was born with a split lower lip it was considered to be a vampire. In Romania, hair on the front or back of a newborn baby was also said to be a sign of vampirism. And in some parts of central Europe, a baby born with visible teeth was believed to be a vampire.

Medieval folklore described several other ways that people could become vampires. One legend said that if a black cat crossed a pregnant woman's path, her baby would be born a vampire. People with red hair and blue eyes in Romania were often suspected to be vampires. In some places it was thought that people could become vampires if they died before being **baptized** as Christians. This could also happen if dead people didn't receive a proper Christian burial.

baptize to pour water on someone as part of a Christian religious practice

FACT: Medieval people sometimes stuffed objects into the mouths of dead bodies to prevent them from becoming vampires. Some of these objects included garlic, soil, gold coins, crosses and even bricks.

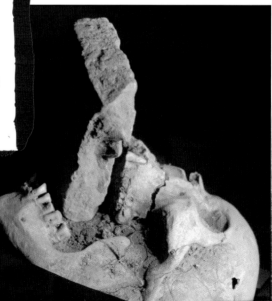

Author Bram Stoker wrote his famous novel *Dracula* in the late 1800s. Stoker based much of his story on European folktales about vampires. But he was also influenced by a terrifying figure from history.

Vlad Tepes, also known as "Vlad the Impaler", was born in Transylvania around 1431. When he grew up, Vlad took the last name of Dracula, which means "son of the dragon". Eventually Vlad became ruler of the region of Walachia, Romania.

Vlad was a brutal leader. He used many horrible punishments against his enemies. His favourite method was to **impale** people on wooden stakes and leave them to die. Vlad soon earned the name of Tepes, or "The Impaler". During his six-year rule, it's thought that he ordered at least 40,000 people to be killed by impaling.

There are no known records of Vlad drinking blood. Some documents state, however, that he enjoyed eating his meals among the bloody, impaled bodies of his victims.

impale to thrust a sharpened stake through a person's body

BLOODTHIRSTY HUNTERS

In many medieval tales, vampires slept in their graves from sunrise to sunset. Bright sunlight supposedly weakened them and their powers. This weakness forced vampires to hunt for blood at night and return to their graves before dawn. But prowling for victims in the dark also helped them to hide their evil deeds.

Several stories stated that vampires were shape-shifters that could take different forms. They could turn into animals such as bats or wolves. Sometimes they could even turn into a misty form and slip under locked doors to reach sleeping victims. Other legends said that vampires couldn't enter a home without first being invited in.

FACT: Greek tales describe vampires called *vrykolakas*. These creatures didn't seek blood like most vampires. They instead spread disease by knocking on people's doors. If someone opened the door after the first knock, the monster would disappear. But the victim would be infected and die within a few days to become a new vrykolakas. For this reason, many people in Greece today refuse to answer the door unless someone knocks twice.

Biting a victim's neck was a common method of vampire attack in many stories. After being bitten, the victim usually went into a **trance**. Without treatment, the victim would waste away and die. Then after a short time, they'd rise from the dead to seek out fresh blood as a newly born vampire.

trance conscious state in which someone is not really aware of what is happening

In the story of Nosferatu, the vampire's victims are unable to resist his supernatural powers.

CHAPTER 3
Medieval monster hunting

Medieval vampires were thought to be ruthless and cunning hunters. However, there were ways that people could protect themselves. Stories were full of defences people could use against the bloodthirsty monsters. The Middle Ages also saw the rise of professional vampire hunters. These highly-skilled people were employed to track down and destroy suspected vampires.

VAMPIRE WEAKNESSES

Vampires in European folklore had several weaknesses. For example, they supposedly hated garlic. To keep vampires away, people often hung strings of garlic around their homes. They also rubbed raw garlic around the windows, doors and chimneys of their homes.

Many medieval people thought that garlic had magical powers against supernatural monsters such as vampires.

People also believed that vampires were evil and unholy creatures. They used holy water or religious symbols, such as Christian **crucifixes**, to drive vampires away.

Vampires were also said to be obsessed with counting things. Several European tales described how people used this weakness to their advantage. They scattered tiny seeds along the road between the graveyard and their homes. They believed that vampires would spend all their time collecting and counting the seeds, rather than hunting for new victims. People often sprinkled seeds or sand around their beds for this same reason.

A Christian crucifix was thought to have the power to defeat a vampire's evil nature.

crucifix   symbol of the beliefs of Christians

HUNTING VAMPIRES

Many people in the Middle Ages believed that professional vampire hunters could help deal with suspected vampires. These hunters often lurked in graveyards at night, looking for signs of vampire activity. If they saw an eerie, blueish light it was considered to be a sign of a **soul** wandering out of its grave. A fresh grave with a hole dug through it was even stronger evidence of vampire activity. And a crooked gravestone or cross could also indicate the presence of a vampire.

soul   spiritual part of a person

Vampire hunters were thought to have the skills needed to track down and destroy evil vampires.

FACT: Some European folklore describes a *dhampir* as the offspring of a vampire and a human. *Dhampirs* made excellent vampire hunters. Being part vampire themselves, they could easily track down evil vampires and destroy them.

Hunters had a few other methods to find vampires. They might scatter salt around the grave of a suspected vampire. If the creature left its grave, it would leave footprints in the salt. Hunters also used animals to detect the undead creatures. Horses were thought to be sensitive to supernatural spirits. If a horse refused to step over a grave, it meant that a vampire could be inside it.

In some stories, vampire hunters used dogs or white wolves to track down suspected vampires.

DESTROYING EVIL VAMPIRES

Hunters in vampire stories had several ways to defend themselves against the evil bloodsuckers. A few hunters carried guns loaded with silver bullets, which were thought to be deadly to a vampire. Hunters also carried containers of holy water, which was believed to burn vampires' flesh.

Medieval people believed that a vampire could be destroyed in several ways. One method involved cutting off the vampire's head. Another was to burn a suspected vampire's body in its grave. But perhaps the best-known method was to drive a wooden stake through the creature's heart.

These methods were also believed to do more than just kill vampires. It was often thought that killing them in this way helped to **redeem** the monsters' souls so they could have a restful death. But according to folklore, even with these methods and defences it was never easy to destroy a vampire. The monsters were almost always alert and ready to fight intruders in their lairs.

redeem to free from the consequences of sinful behaviour

FACT: In 1486 the Christian church published a book called *Malleus Maleficarium*. It described how vampires were connected to the devil. The book also provided advice for how to deal with the demonic creatures. By the 1600s the *Malleus Maleficarium* became a guidebook for vampire hunters across Europe.

Medieval tales about vampire hunters were probably the inspiration for the most famous vampire hunter of all time. Professor Abraham Van Helsing was the main hunter in Bram Stoker's famous novel *Dracula*. Van Helsing set the standard for how vampire hunters are portrayed in many modern films, TV series and books.

Van Helsing was very intelligent and used several vampire hunting tools. As well as garlic, holy water and a crucifix, he also carried a mirror to learn a vampire's true nature. In the story, vampires had no soul, so they had no reflection in the mirror. Van Helsing's tool kit also included a wooden stake and hammer.

A vampire hunter's kit included several weapons such as crucifixes, holy water, a mirror and wooden stakes.

CHAPTER 4
Vampires today

People have long been fascinated with tales of gruesome vampires. But the image of these dynamic monsters has changed over time. While they were once portrayed as evil and bloodthirsty monsters, vampires in today's stories are often seen as heroes.

EARLY WRITINGS

In 1819, British physician John Polidori wrote one of the first popular vampire books. Simply titled *The Vampyre*, it featured Lord Ruthven, a dashing nobleman who hungered for blood. Ruthven used his natural charm to gain people's trust. But when people let him into their homes, he would attack them violently.

Another popular early novel was *Varney the Vampire: or The Feast of Blood*. James Malcolm Rymer wrote this novel in 1847. Varney was the first vampire with several classic vampire traits. He is described as being tall, ugly and very pale. He also has long fangs and fingernails. He often attacks women and even turns some of them into vampires. The novel became very popular, and Varney would later have a strong influence on the most popular vampire story of all time.

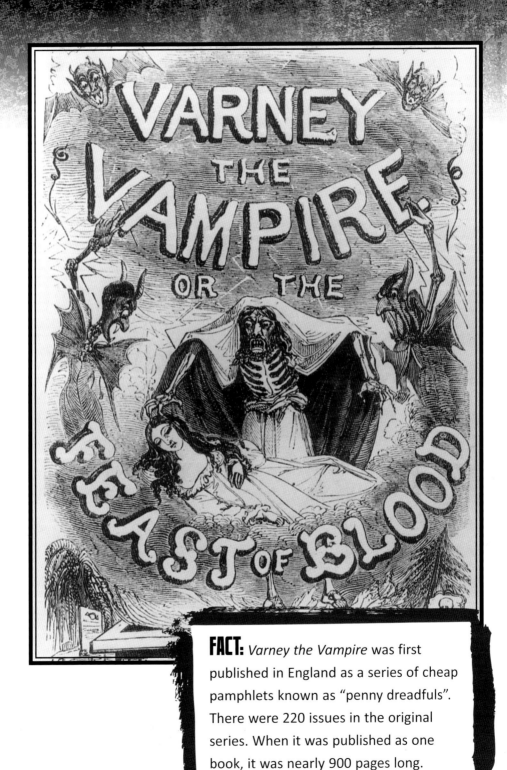

FACT: *Varney the Vampire* was first published in England as a series of cheap pamphlets known as "penny dreadfuls". There were 220 issues in the original series. When it was published as one book, it was nearly 900 pages long.

DRACULA

Bram Stoker's 1897 book *Dracula* is the most famous vampire story ever written. The character of Count Dracula has strongly influenced vampires in books, films and TV series for more than 100 years. Dracula's powers and abilities captured people's imaginations. Because he has no soul, he doesn't have a shadow and has no reflection in mirrors. He has the power to control nature and the ability to scale castle walls. Even daylight doesn't harm him. But Dracula has to sleep in his native Transylvanian soil to maintain his powers.

Bram Stoker was inspired by the ruined abbey and graveyard in Whitby, Yorkshire. Part of his novel Dracula *is set in this small town.*

Stoker's novel brought more attention to vampires than any previous story. Dracula soon became the model upon which most authors based their vampires. Many vampires in modern tales have the same powers and abilities as Count Dracula.

FACT: In Stoker's novel, Count Dracula appears quite ugly. He has hairy palms, bad breath and wears strange clothing. But his appearance later changed in films and stage plays. In the 1931 film *Dracula*, he is a smartly dressed and sophisticated nobleman.

EVOLUTION OF THE VAMPIRE

In many modern books, films and TV series, vampires have become heroes. They are concerned about the safety of their human friends and are able to hold back their evil natures. They want to "do the right thing" in spite of being vampires. For example, they often choose to drink animal blood instead of attacking humans.

Modern vampires are also often more attractive than the gruesome monsters of the past. They don't have claws or fangs. They wear normal clothes and don't look like **corpses**. Modern vampires also don't seem to age. They instead seem to stay young and good-looking forever.

corpse dead body

The TV series Angel *featured a vampire who had regained his soul. He fought to protect innocent people from bloodthirsty vampires and other evil creatures.*

FACT: Sunlight doesn't hurt vampires in many modern stories. The creatures just look very pale instead. Sometimes they may wear dark cloaks or sunglasses.

Although a few modern vampires are heroic, many others are still evil. They are dark and soulless creatures. These evil vampires are often cunning and always dangerous. They'll stop at nothing to get the blood and power they want. In most of these stories, heroic vampires are often the only ones able to stop evil vampires' wicked plans.

VAMPIRES THROUGH THE AGES

From ancient tales to modern pop culture, vampires have played an important role in our stories. While vampires have always had a dark side, they have appeared differently over time. They're often terrifying creatures that attack people to satisfy their hunger for blood. But sometimes they're seen as good-looking heroes who fight to protect humans.

Unlike people in ancient or medieval times, we no longer believe that vampires are real creatures. But people today still enjoy being scared by these bloodsucking monsters. New books about vampires are often best-sellers. And cinemas are often packed with vampire fans who want to see the latest hit film. It seems that no matter how terrifying they are, people can't get enough of their favourite bloodsucking monsters.

FACT: In the 1960s the TV series *The Munsters* showed vampires living like normal people. Count Vladimir Dracula, also known as Grandpa Munster, was a scientist. But he was also a 378-year-old vampire with a pet Transylvanian bat called Igor. His daughter Lily was also a vampire. She spent her days as a housewife and mother.

VAMPIRES IN POPULAR CULTURE

TITLE	GOOD/EVIL	MEDIA	YEAR
Nosferatu	evil	film	1922
Dracula	evil	film	1931
The Addams Family	good	TV	1964–1966
The Munsters	good	TV	1964–1966
Dark Shadows	both	TV	1966–1971
The Monster Squad	evil	film	1987
Buffy the Vampire Slayer	both	TV	1997–2003
Castlevania	evil	video game	1999
Angel	both	TV	1999–2004
Twilight	both	novels/films	2005–2012
Hotel Transylvania	good	film	2012

In Buffy the Vampire Slayer, Spike first appears as an evil vampire. But over time he becomes a hero.

Glossary

baptize to pour water on someone as part of a Christian religious practice

corpse dead body

crucifix symbol of the beliefs of Christians

decompose to rot or decay

folklore tales, sayings and customs among a group of people

hypnotize to put a person into a sleep-like state

impale to thrust a sharpened stake through a person's body

medieval having to do with the period of European history between AD 500 and 1450

plague disease that spreads quickly and kills most people who catch it

redeem to free from the consequences of sinful behaviour

soul spiritual part of a person

trance conscious state in which a person is not really aware of what is happening

undead no longer alive but still able to move and take action

Books

The Vampire Hunter's Guide (Monster Tracker)
Otto De'Ath (Franklin Watts, 2012)

Vampires and Werewolves (Solving Mysteries with Science),
Jane Bingham (Raintree, 2014)

Vampires vs. Werewolves: Battle of the Bloodthirsty Beasts
(Monster Wars), Michael O'Hearn (Raintree, 2012)

Websites

www.listverse.com/2010/09/30/8-vampire-myths-explained/
Learn the truth behind several popular myths about vampires.

www.mysteriousbritain.co.uk/folklore/vampire-folklore.html
Learn about vampire myths and folklore in the United Kingdom.

www.pantheon.org/articles/v/vampire.html
Discover more about the history behind vampire myths.

Index